A-SHOPPING I WILL GO

People To Buy For:

☐ _____   ☐ _____

☐ _____   ☐ _____

☐ _____   ☐ _____

☐ _____   ☐ _____

☐ _____   ☐ _____

☐ _____   ☐ _____

☐ _____   ☐ _____

☐ _____   ☐ _____

☐ _____   ☐ _____

☐ _____   ☐ _____

☐ _____   ☐ _____

☐ _____   ☐ _____

☐ _____   ☐ _____

People To Buy For:

☐ _____   ☐ _____

☐ _____   ☐ _____

☐ _____   ☐ _____

☐ _____   ☐ _____

☐ _____   ☐ _____

☐ _____   ☐ _____

☐ _____   ☐ _____

☐ _____   ☐ _____

☐ _____   ☐ _____

☐ _____   ☐ _____

☐ _____   ☐ _____

☐ _____   ☐ _____

☐ _____   ☐ _____

Name:

_____

Gift Ideas:

_____

_____

_____

_____

Sizes/Notes:

_____

_____

_____

_____

_____

❏ Gift/Gifts Purchased _____

_____

❏ Amount Spent _____

❏ Purchased From _____

❏ On _____

Notes

Name:

_____

Gift Ideas:

_____

_____

_____

_____

Sizes/Notes:

_____

_____

_____

_____

_____

❑ Gift/Gifts Purchased _____

_____

❑ Amount Spent _____

❑ Purchased From _____

❑ On _____

Notes

Name:

_____

Gift Ideas:

_____
_____
_____
_____

Sizes/Notes:

_____
_____
_____
_____
_____

❑ Gift/Gifts Purchased _____

_____

❑ Amount Spent _____

❑ Purchased From _____

❑ On _____

Notes

Name:

_____

Gift Ideas:

_____

_____

_____

_____

Sizes/Notes:

_____

_____

_____

_____

_____

❑ Gift/Gifts Purchased _____

_____

❑ Amount Spent _____

❑ Purchased From _____

❑ On _____

Notes

Name:

_____

Gift Ideas:

_____

_____

_____

_____

Sizes/Notes:

_____

_____

_____

_____

❏ Gift/Gifts Purchased _____

_____

❏ Amount Spent _____

❏ Purchased From _____

❏ On _____

Notes

Name:

_____

Gift Ideas:

_____

_____

_____

_____

Sizes/Notes:

_____

_____

_____

_____

_____

❑ Gift/Gifts Purchased _____

_____

❑ Amount Spent _____

❑ Purchased From _____

❑ On _____

Notes

Name:

_____

Gift Ideas:

_____

_____

_____

_____

Sizes/Notes:

_____

_____

_____

_____

_____

❑ Gift/Gifts Purchased _____

_____

❑ Amount Spent _____

❑ Purchased From _____

❑ On _____

Notes

Name:

_____

Gift Ideas:

_____
_____
_____
_____

Sizes/Notes:

_____
_____
_____
_____
_____

❑ Gift/Gifts Purchased _____

_____

❑ Amount Spent _____

❑ Purchased From _____

❑ On _____

Notes

Name:

_____

Gift Ideas:

_____

_____

_____

_____

Sizes/Notes:

_____

_____

_____

_____

_____

❑ Gift/Gifts Purchased _____

_____

❑ Amount Spent _____

❑ Purchased From _____

❑ On _____

Notes

Name:

_____

Gift Ideas:

_____

_____

_____

_____

Sizes/Notes:

_____

_____

_____

_____

_____

❑ Gift/Gifts Purchased _____

_____

❑ Amount Spent _____

❑ Purchased From _____

❑ On _____

Notes

Name:

_____

Gift Ideas:

_____
_____
_____
_____

Sizes/Notes:

_____
_____
_____
_____
_____

❑ Gift/Gifts Purchased _____

_____

❑ Amount Spent _____

❑ Purchased From _____

❑ On _____

Notes

Name:

_____

Gift Ideas:

_____
_____
_____
_____

Sizes/Notes:

_____
_____
_____
_____
_____

❑ Gift/Gifts Purchased _____

_____

❑ Amount Spent _____

❑ Purchased From _____

❑ On _____

Notes

Name:

_____

Gift Ideas:

_____

_____

_____

_____

Sizes/Notes:

_____

_____

_____

_____

_____

❑ Gift/Gifts Purchased _____

_____

❑ Amount Spent _____

❑ Purchased From _____

❑ On _____

Notes

Name:

_____

Gift Ideas:

_____

_____

_____

_____

Sizes/Notes:

_____

_____

_____

_____

_____

❑ Gift/Gifts Purchased _____

_____

❑ Amount Spent _____

❑ Purchased From _____

❑ On _____

Notes

Name:

_____

Gift Ideas:

_____

_____

_____

_____

Sizes/Notes:

_____

_____

_____

_____

_____

❑ Gift/Gifts Purchased _____

_____

❑ Amount Spent _____

❑ Purchased From _____

❑ On _____

Notes

Name:

_____

Gift Ideas:

_____

_____

_____

_____

Sizes/Notes:

_____

_____

_____

_____

❑ Gift/Gifts Purchased _____

_____

❑ Amount Spent _____

❑ Purchased From _____

❑ On _____

Notes

Name:

_____

Gift Ideas:

_____
_____
_____
_____

Sizes/Notes:

_____
_____
_____
_____
_____

❑ Gift/Gifts Purchased _____

_____

❑ Amount Spent _____

❑ Purchased From _____

❑ On _____

Notes

Name:

_____

Gift Ideas:

_____
_____
_____
_____

Sizes/Notes:

_____
_____
_____
_____
_____

❑ Gift/Gifts Purchased _____

_____

❑ Amount Spent _____

❑ Purchased From _____

❑ On _____

Notes

Name:

_____

Gift Ideas:

_____

_____

_____

_____

Sizes/Notes:

_____

_____

_____

_____

❑ Gift/Gifts Purchased _____

_____

❑ Amount Spent _____

❑ Purchased From _____

❑ On _____

Notes

Name:

_____

Gift Ideas:

_____

_____

_____

_____

Sizes/Notes:

_____

_____

_____

_____

_____

❑ Gift/Gifts Purchased _____

_____

❑ Amount Spent _____

❑ Purchased From _____

❑ On _____

Notes

Name:

_____

Gift Ideas:

_____
_____
_____
_____

Sizes/Notes:

_____
_____
_____
_____
_____

❑ Gift/Gifts Purchased _____

_____

❑ Amount Spent _____

❑ Purchased From _____

❑ On _____

Notes

Name:

_____

Gift Ideas:

_____

_____

_____

_____

Sizes/Notes:

_____

_____

_____

_____

_____

❏ Gift/Gifts Purchased _____

_____

❏ Amount Spent _____

❏ Purchased From _____

❏ On _____

Notes

Name:

_____

Gift Ideas:

_____
_____
_____
_____

Sizes/Notes:

_____
_____
_____
_____
_____

❑ Gift/Gifts Purchased _____

_____

❑ Amount Spent _____

❑ Purchased From _____

❑ On _____

Notes

Name:

_____

Gift Ideas:

_____

_____

_____

_____

Sizes/Notes:

_____

_____

_____

_____

_____

❑ Gift/Gifts Purchased _____

_____

❑ Amount Spent _____

❑ Purchased From _____

❑ On _____

Notes

Name:

_____

Gift Ideas:

_____
_____
_____
_____

Sizes/Notes:

_____
_____
_____
_____

❑ Gift/Gifts Purchased _____

_____

❑ Amount Spent _____

❑ Purchased From _____

❑ On _____

Notes

Name:

_____

Gift Ideas:

_____

_____

_____

_____

Sizes/Notes:

_____

_____

_____

_____

❑ Gift/Gifts Purchased _____

_____

❑ Amount Spent _____

❑ Purchased From _____

❑ On _____

Notes

Name:

_____

Gift Ideas:

_____
_____
_____
_____

Sizes/Notes:

_____
_____
_____
_____
_____

❑ Gift/Gifts Purchased _____

_____

❑ Amount Spent _____

❑ Purchased From _____

❑ On _____

Notes

Name:

_____

Gift Ideas:

_____

_____

_____

_____

Sizes/Notes:

_____

_____

_____

_____

_____

❑ Gift/Gifts Purchased _____

_____

❑ Amount Spent _____

❑ Purchased From _____

❑ On _____

Notes

Name:

_____

Gift Ideas:

_____

_____

_____

_____

Sizes/Notes:

_____

_____

_____

_____

_____

❑ Gift/Gifts Purchased _____

_____

❑ Amount Spent _____

❑ Purchased From _____

❑ On _____

Notes

Name:

_____

Gift Ideas:

_____
_____
_____
_____

Sizes/Notes:

_____
_____
_____
_____
_____

❑ Gift/Gifts Purchased _____

_____

❑ Amount Spent _____

❑ Purchased From _____

❑ On _____

Notes

Name:

_____

Gift Ideas:

_____

_____

_____

_____

Sizes/Notes:

_____

_____

_____

_____

❑ Gift/Gifts Purchased _____

_____

❑ Amount Spent _____

❑ Purchased From _____

❑ On _____

Notes

Name:

_____

Gift Ideas:

_____
_____
_____
_____

Sizes/Notes:

_____
_____
_____
_____
_____

❑ Gift/Gifts Purchased _____

_____

❑ Amount Spent _____

❑ Purchased From _____

❑ On _____

Notes

Name:

_____

Gift Ideas:

_____

_____

_____

_____

Sizes/Notes:

_____

_____

_____

_____

_____

❑ Gift/Gifts Purchased _____

_____

❑ Amount Spent _____

❑ Purchased From _____

❑ On _____

Notes

Name:

_____

Gift Ideas:

_____
_____
_____
_____

Sizes/Notes:

_____
_____
_____
_____
_____

❑ Gift/Gifts Purchased _____

_____

❑ Amount Spent _____

❑ Purchased From _____

❑ On _____

Notes

Name:

_____

Gift Ideas:

_____
_____
_____
_____

Sizes/Notes:

_____
_____
_____
_____
_____

❑ Gift/Gifts Purchased _____

_____

❑ Amount Spent _____

❑ Purchased From _____

❑ On _____

Notes

Name:

_____

Gift Ideas:

_____
_____
_____
_____

Sizes/Notes:

_____
_____
_____
_____
_____

❑ Gift/Gifts Purchased _____

_____

❑ Amount Spent _____

❑ Purchased From _____

❑ On _____

Notes

Name:

_____

Gift Ideas:

_____

_____

_____

_____

Sizes/Notes:

_____

_____

_____

_____

_____

❑ Gift/Gifts Purchased _____

_____

❑ Amount Spent _____

❑ Purchased From _____

❑ On _____

Notes

Name:

_____

Gift Ideas:

_____
_____
_____
_____

Sizes/Notes:

_____
_____
_____
_____
_____

❑ Gift/Gifts Purchased _____

_____

❑ Amount Spent _____

❑ Purchased From _____

❑ On _____

Notes

Name:

_____

Gift Ideas:

_____

_____

_____

_____

Sizes/Notes:

_____

_____

_____

_____

_____

❑ Gift/Gifts Purchased _____

_____

❑ Amount Spent _____

❑ Purchased From _____

❑ On _____

Notes

Name:

_____

Gift Ideas:

_____

_____

_____

_____

Sizes/Notes:

_____

_____

_____

_____

_____

❑ Gift/Gifts Purchased _____

_____

❑ Amount Spent _____

❑ Purchased From _____

❑ On _____

Notes

Name:

_____

Gift Ideas:

_____
_____
_____
_____

Sizes/Notes:

_____
_____
_____
_____
_____

❑ Gift/Gifts Purchased _____

_____

❑ Amount Spent _____

❑ Purchased From _____

❑ On _____

Notes

Name:

_____

Gift Ideas:

_____

_____

_____

_____

Sizes/Notes:

_____

_____

_____

_____

_____

❑ Gift/Gifts Purchased _____

_____

❑ Amount Spent _____

❑ Purchased From _____

❑ On _____

Notes

Name:

_____

Gift Ideas:

_____
_____
_____
_____

Sizes/Notes:

_____
_____
_____
_____
_____

❑ Gift/Gifts Purchased _____

_____

❑ Amount Spent _____

❑ Purchased From _____

❑ On _____

Notes

Name:

_____

Gift Ideas:

_____
_____
_____
_____

Sizes/Notes:

_____
_____
_____
_____
_____

❑ Gift/Gifts Purchased _____

_____

❑ Amount Spent _____

❑ Purchased From _____

❑ On _____

Notes

Name:

_____

Gift Ideas:

_____

_____

_____

_____

Sizes/Notes:

_____

_____

_____

_____

_____

❑ Gift/Gifts Purchased _____

_____

❑ Amount Spent _____

❑ Purchased From _____

❑ On _____

Notes

Name:

_____

Gift Ideas:

_____

_____

_____

_____

Sizes/Notes:

_____

_____

_____

_____

❑ Gift/Gifts Purchased _____

_____

❑ Amount Spent _____

❑ Purchased From _____

❑ On _____

Notes

Name:

_____

Gift Ideas:

_____
_____
_____
_____

Sizes/Notes:

_____
_____
_____
_____
_____

❑ Gift/Gifts Purchased _____

_____

❑ Amount Spent _____

❑ Purchased From _____

❑ On _____

Notes

Name:

_____

Gift Ideas:

_____
_____
_____
_____

Sizes/Notes:

_____
_____
_____
_____
_____

❑ Gift/Gifts Purchased _____

_____

❑ Amount Spent _____

❑ Purchased From _____

❑ On _____

Notes

Name:

_____

Gift Ideas:

_____
_____
_____
_____

Sizes/Notes:

_____
_____
_____
_____
_____

❑ Gift/Gifts Purchased _____

_____

❑ Amount Spent _____

❑ Purchased From _____

❑ On _____

Notes

Name:

_____

Gift Ideas:

_____

_____

_____

_____

Sizes/Notes:

_____

_____

_____

_____

_____

❑ Gift/Gifts Purchased _____

_____

❑ Amount Spent _____

❑ Purchased From _____

❑ On _____

Notes

Name:

_____

Gift Ideas:

_____

_____

_____

_____

Sizes/Notes:

_____

_____

_____

_____

_____

❑ Gift/Gifts Purchased _____

_____

❑ Amount Spent _____

❑ Purchased From _____

❑ On _____

Notes

Name:

_____

Gift Ideas:

_____
_____
_____
_____

Sizes/Notes:

_____
_____
_____
_____
_____

❑ Gift/Gifts Purchased _____

_____

❑ Amount Spent _____

❑ Purchased From _____

❑ On _____

Notes

Name:

_____

Gift Ideas:

_____

_____

_____

_____

Sizes/Notes:

_____

_____

_____

_____

_____

❑ Gift/Gifts Purchased _____

_____

❑ Amount Spent _____

❑ Purchased From _____

❑ On _____

Notes

Made in the USA
Coppell, TX
21 November 2020